THE **COLOUR** OF **CANADA**

THE
COLOUR
OF CANADA

TEXT BY ROY MacGREGOR

McCLELLAND & STEWART

CONTENTS

INTRODUCTION

"Where am I?"

It was the strangest feeling of all – one of complete and utter insignificance, of being so small that one was no longer matter in any sense of the word. A pinhole in a clean sheet of paper would have seemed colossal by comparison. It was like slipping into another world where nothing whatsoever is the same as the world just left – and yet both worlds were still ... Canada.

We were in a de Havilland Twin Otter, an aircraft that had been built before Captain Dominique Lassonde, the National Defence pilot at the controls, was even born. It was the middle of June 2005, and Captain Lassonde was flying the then governor general, Adrienne Clarkson, her husband, John Ralston Saul, two aides, a photographer, and a journalist between Base Alert, on the northern tip of Ellesmere Island, and the Eureka weather station, located several hours by air to the south and west but still very much in the High Arctic.

It would be this governor general's final trip to the Far North before her time in office came to an end, and she intended the visit as a political statement on sovereignty – her country's claim on distant extremities of the national body that most Canadians don't even know are there.

There is nothing condescending in such a statement, for I stand with those Canadians. At one point during this long journey through the North we had passed over a massive string of mountains I had neither seen nor heard of – the United States Range. Immediately to the west of these behemoths that would rival the Rockies stood the vast British Empire Range, another curiously named mountain range of which I was blissfully unaware.

Where did they *come from?*

The noisy, cramped Twin Otter slowly worked its way south along the east coast of Ellesmere Island before turning inland. Here the plane would follow Archer Fiord as it plunged deep into the huge island. From the end of the fjord we would catch the path of the Dodge River, following its twisting course inland until eventually reaching one of the great ice fields of the High Arctic.

It was a perfect, sunny day in this brief season of twenty-four-hour light. Every so often the plane would pass over melting ice sitting in pools of water, the reflection the magnificent polar azure that, on a fine sunny summer day, turns the Arctic landscape into one of the most beautiful places on earth.

Captain Lassonde chose the lowest flight path the Twin Otter could safely navigate, flying along the fjord

Military base CFS Alert, Ellesmere Island, Nunavut

as if the plane were floating between the towering black-shadowed cliffs on both sides. We were all hooked up by intercom – a necessary safety feature in the noisy aircraft – so we could not only hear flight information coming from the cockpit but also exchange comments among ourselves. The expressions of incredulity simply steamrolled over each other as the plane rose and turned and twisted through the fjord and then along the river path, mountains rising sharply on both sides.

I was sitting in the co-pilot's seat – an unimaginable treat – when suddenly Captain Lassonde pulled back on the controls and the Twin Otter roared and rose out of the river valley, gracefully up and past the cliffs until it was over a spreading plateau of pure, blinding white that seemed to go on forever.

My earphones suddenly filled with random expressions of delight:

"So beautiful!"

"Awesome!"

Not "awesome" as in what the young waitress says when you add chicken strips to your Caesar salad, but "awesome" in its proper meaning: daunting, awe-inspiring, breathtaking, staggering . . .

And then, just as quickly, the intercom of the Twin Otter went silent.

It was the strangest of all imaginable experiences. From feeling like we were travelling through the veins of Ellesmere, we suddenly rose over a world so deep and distant and starkly white, bare eyes could not look at it. The plane, which had somehow seemed so significant, in charge even, as it had roared along, twisting over the gorges and above the riverbed with its fractured ice and blue reflections, now took on an *insignificance* that was unexpected and remains inexplicable.

The plane seemed to shrink, now little more than a mosquito flying over a vast white shoulder of a country with more than thirty-three million citizens, perhaps none of whom had ever set foot on the expansive territory we were looking down upon.

No one in the plane spoke. No one *dared* speak, each passenger and crew member struck by his or her minuteness in a land so large and diverse neither words nor art nor photography, nor even the imagination, seem capable of capturing it wholly.

I remember vividly my own silent feelings at that moment.

Where am I?

I thought I knew this country – yet the sense of . . . well, *ignorance* . . . was almost overwhelming. In an instant, such a thought had turned into an impossible conceit, a foolish arrogance.

Perhaps you could never fully know this country.

This year, 2017, marks the sesqui-centennial of Canada. It is a remarkable year in that it is also the one-hundredth anniversary of Vimy Ridge, the pivotal First World War battle that helped Canadians see inside themselves, and one hundred years since the death of Tom Thomson, the landscape artist who opened the eyes of Canadians to what was outside. All three events will be saluted throughout 2017.

It may entirely pass notice that this will also be the seventy-fifth anniversary of the publication of Bruce Hutchison's epic *The Unknown Country*. Forgotten today, it was for many years the best-known book in the land, its opening paragraph both lyrical and haunting:

> No one knows my country, neither the stranger nor its own sons. My country has not found itself nor felt its power nor learned its true place. It is all visions and doubts and hopes and dreams. It is strength and weakness, despair and joy, and the wild confusions and restless strivings of a boy who has passed his boyhood but is not yet a man.

Not surprisingly, Hutchison's iconic publication reads rather out of date today in such matters as gender equality and political correctness, but his observation that this was but an adolescent country seventy-five

"Perhaps you could never fully know this country."

years after Confederation was apt. Just as a young man or woman stares into the future with excitement and uncertainty, Hutchison's Canada was then seemingly just starting out. There were but eleven million citizens, a third of today's population, with almost all of them huddled around the lights of their communities along the southern borders – the country, like the future during this time of war in which he was writing, seemingly forever beyond.

"All about us lies Canada," Hutchison wrote, "forever untouched, unknown, beyond our grasp, breathing deep in the darkness and we hear its breath and are afraid. . . . No, they could not know us, the strangers, for we have not known ourselves."

It was William Lyon Mackenzie King, the tenth prime minister of Canada, who said that this country has "too much geography and not

Lake Hazen, northern Ellesmere Island, Nunavut

enough history." King was prime minister when Hutchison was somewhat reluctantly writing *The Unknown Country* (a New York publisher had talked him into it during a lunch that involved more alcohol than Hutchison was used to imbibing). Today, Hutchison's subject is twice as old as it was then, the population three times as great – yet geography still trumps history.

It's prohibitively expensive to travel this country the way one can Europe or the United States. Flights are costly, distances off-putting, much of the land inaccessible except by helicopter, float plane, canoe, or kayak. I have been blessed to spend more than four decades as a journalist in this "unknown country," lucky to have a career travelling about Canada writing about its sports, politicians, people, and places – and fortunate beyond belief to have someone with deeper pockets than mine pay for most of it. When this particular cheapskate travels on his own dollar, it more often than not involves transportation by water, shelter by tent.

Thanks to the sheer luck of career, I have stood at Cape Spear in Newfoundland as the first sunlight of the twenty-first century spread across the Atlantic Ocean and washed over Canadian shores. I have waded into the Pacific Ocean at Tofino, on Vancouver Island, and body surfed back to shore. During that 2005 trip north with the then

GG, Adrienne Clarkson, I was able to stand at the very end of the long runway at Alert and stare across the fields of broken ice knowing that around the earth's curve lay Russia.

And that merely covers the three oceans, quick notes from three extremely small strips of the astonishing 265,523 kilometres of shoreline that the World Resources Institute says this country covers. This measurement means that approximately one sixth of the time the world's salt water is in direct contact with land, it is with Canadian land. We have vastly more shoreline than the United States, which ranks second with roughly half the coast Canada claims, and more again than third-ranked Russia.

Within the confines of such watery borders, I have been fortunate enough to see flax bloom like a blue sea in Saskatchewan, while on another trip I gazed upon the same field turned completely white with tens of thousands of snow geese on their spring migration north. I've seen salmon swimming in the Miramichi, watched water thunder over Kakabeka Falls in northwestern Ontario, and stared in wonder while imagining an ancient Blackfoot hunt at Head-Smashed-In Buffalo Jump near Fort Macleod, Alberta.

Friends joke that I may have seen more of the country than anyone. That's obviously an unmeasurable achievement, but I have seen a great deal of Canada, much of it as a lone

Pembina Hills, Manitoba

wolf travelling, often weeks at a time, during federal and provincial elections, Royal Tours, Olympic torch relays, and hockey and curling tournaments, not to mention those seemingly annual newspaper and magazine assignments that are usually referred to as "taking the pulse of the nation." More accurately, you take "snapshots," true perhaps for the moment but hardly all-knowing or fully-understanding. The lens has yet to be invented that can capture an entire province let alone the entire country.

The more I've seen, the more I'm aware of what has not been seen and, let's face it, what will never be seen. I understand why David Thompson, the great mapmaker who travelled some eighty thousand kilometres by foot, horse, and canoe, would believe that he had seen but a small fraction of the land that lay out there farther than any eye can see.

Thompson died at the age of eighty-seven in 1857, born before the first trains, dead decades before auto-mobiles and planes. I have had the advantage of travelling two million air miles on Air Canada (according to a recent twenty-fifth-anniversary note from Aeroplan), hundreds of thousands of miles and kilometres on other airlines, plus many more by train, helicopter, bush plane, rental car, motorcycle, and thumb, as well as various types and sizes of water-craft. Despite his obvious travel restrictions, David Thompson still

mapped 3.1 million square kilometres of the land that, ten years after his passing, would become Canada, a country that today, at 150 years old, includes ten provinces and three territories, covering some 9.85 million square kilometres.

In other words, David Thompson didn't know the half of it – and knew he didn't.

I thought of David Thompson as I leafed through the spectacular photographs assembled for *The Colour of Canada*. As well as his necessary guides, paddlers, and supplies; his wife, Charlotte Small; and whatever number of their eventual thirteen children were along for the ride, Thompson carried with him a sense of wonder about his chosen country that never left him. This wonder is found regularly in his journals. "At length the Rocky Mountains came in sight like shining white clouds on the horizon," he wrote when his long trek across the prairie was nearing its end, "but we doubted what our guide said; but as we proceeded, they rose in height, their immense masses of snow appeared above the clouds, and formed an impassable barrier, even to the Eagle."

Thompson eventually made it over that "impassable barrier" and, after one time-consuming false start, followed the Columbia River all the way to its mouth at the Pacific. He would, therefore, have seen many of the same mountains contained in this book – though none had a "Skywalk" such as the one that hangs over the Columbia Icefield not far from Banff. He would have seen the northern lights, the heather and glacier lily found in the alpine meadows above the treeline, the great roaring rivers of the West – and he would have seen it all by foot and by canoe.

How appropriate, then, that the canoe would be featured in this book, a simple, empty canoe that seems to be awaiting a paddler to head out into this endlessly fascinating landscape. How nice, as well, that it is red, as a red canoe hangs in our garage and a red canoe awaits at the small cabin near Ontario's Algonquin Park where my family spends as much of our summers as possible. I feel particularly partial to the canoe, as I have long believed, "No canoe; no Canada." Or, perhaps better put by legendary paddler and outdoors filmmaker Bill Mason: "First God created a canoe – then He created a country to go with it."

In the spring of 2007, the CBC launched a contest to identify "The Seven Wonders of Canada." I was one of three jurors – along with lawyer and First Nations activist Roberta Jamieson and Ra McGuire of the rock band Trooper – and it fell to us to winnow down the fifty-two nominations to seven wonders. There were the obvious choices – Peggy's

Cove, the Rockies, Niagara Falls – as well as such familiar landmarks as Gros Morne National Park, the Cypress Hills, the Cabot Trail, and Haida Gwaii. Cities were also well represented – the CN Tower, Old Quebec, the Manitoba legislature, Stanley Park – as were such emotional objects as the Vimy Memorial and the Stanley Cup.

More than a million CBC listeners and viewers cast votes, and then the three judges went to work, arguing and defending while *The National* filmed. The list was eventually pared to fifteen: the Bay of Fundy, the Cabot Trail, Cathedral Grove, Gros Morne, Haida Gwaii, the Nahanni River, Niagara Falls, the northern lights, Old Quebec, Pier 21, prairie skies, the Sleeping Giant, the Rockies, the igloo, and the canoe. It fell to me to argue the case for the canoe. Knowing the Canadian propensity for political correctness, I calculated that *geographical* correctness would also come into play before this exercise was over, so I suggested that the beauty of the canoe was that it had no location but could be found everywhere across the country. In some ways the canoe was most symbolic of all, as it alone covered both history and geography and was, therefore, the greatest wonder of a wonderful country. When Peter Mansbridge announced the seven winners, first up was the canoe.

The others chosen as the Seven Wonders of Canada were the Rockies

"...a simple, empty canoe that seems to be awaiting a paddler to head out into this endlessly fascinating landscape"

and Niagara Falls – how could they possibly not be on the list? – prairie skies, the igloo, and two special areas from Canadian cities, Old Quebec and Halifax's Pier 21, the latter welcoming more than one million immigrants in the early decades of the twentieth century.

When we first think of a book of Canadian photographs, we immediately consider the obvious clichés – Mounties and moose – but also those landscapes that shout "Canada" to us and to the world. There are, as there must be, exquisite photographs here of prairie fields, mountains, coastlines, lighthouses, grain elevators, churches, farms, covered bridges, northern lights, icebergs, and trains. But there are

Head Lake, Algonquin Park, Ontario

also magnificent portraits of our cities and their special spots that have become part of what Canadians think of when they consider their favourite landscapes. Who has visited St. John's and failed to stand on Signal Hill and look down upon that magnificent harbour? If you go to Winnipeg, you head for The Forks to find peace and quiet, perhaps adding in a stop at the Canadian Museum for Human Rights, surely the most intriguing architectural feat this country has seen over the past decade. Thunder Bay has its famous harbour, with a perfect view of the distant rock formation that is known as the Sleeping Giant.

Montreal has the energy and excitement of rue Sainte-Catherine, with the green solitude of Mount Royal but a short walk away. Toronto has the sizzle of Yonge Street and the cool greens of its many ravines and nearby islands. Every city in the country has its special place – Edmonton's River Valley, Quebec City's ramparts, Calgary's Eau Claire Market, Fredericton's Beaverbrook Art Gallery, Regina's legislature and Wascana Centre, Vancouver's Granville Island, Charlottetown's *Anne of Green Gables* musical at Confederation Centre of the Arts. Ottawa has its pomp and ceremony on Parliament Hill for summer, the world's largest skating rink for winter.

Travelling this country as a journalist has also taken me past the giant paperclip at Kipling, SK; the giant hockey stick in Duncan, BC; the giant goose at Wawa, ON; the giant lobster at Shediac, NB; the giant Inuksuk at Inuvik, NWT; the giant chair at Springbank, NL; the giant curling stone at Arborg, MB; the giant whales at Tadoussac, QC; the giant wave in Halifax, NS; the giant cow at Cavendish, PEI; the two-storey outhouse at Whitehorse, Yukon; and Squirt, the giant skunk who presides over the town park in little Beiseker, AB.

There is humour to be found out there, for sure, but also sadness. You can feel it as you stand by the statue that graces the Trans-Canada Highway near Thunder Bay, where Terry Fox stopped on August 21, 1980, cancer ending his Marathon of Hope, but never to end his inspiration to others. You can read it in, of all places, the library of the University of Saskatchewan Law School in Saskatoon, where a glass case holds an old fender in which, on June 8, 1948, a Rosetown farmer, pinned in wet clay by his overturned tractor, scratched his final will, sixteen words long, with a pocket knife: "In case I die in this mess I leave all to the wife. Cecil Geo Harris." The will, just in case you were wondering, stood up in court, which is why the law school treasures it.

You can sense an overwhelming sorrow in your bones if you take the ferry out from Berthier-sur-Mer to Grosse Île near the throat of the St. Lawrence River, where 5,424 Irish

Canada Goose statue, Wawa, Ontario

lie in mass graves. Included in that shocking number are ten Mary Kellys – likely infant Mary Kellys, young Mary Kellys, mother Mary Kellys, grandmother Mary Kellys. The Mary Kellys died during the summer and fall of 1847, when some hundred thousand desperate Irish fled the potato famine and nearly four hundred ships put into the Grosse Île harbour, where they were quarantined until medical officials could decide which passengers were free of typhus and could be given permission to continue on to Quebec City. Those passengers who arrived dead or dying never left Grosse Île, their bodies piled together in deep holes and covered over without so much as a marking. Today, Parks Canada keeps the fields where the dead were laid to rest perfectly manicured, a large Celtic cross standing in their honour on a high cliff near the approach to the harbour.

I came to Grosse Île on a blustery day in 2015, just starting out on a *Globe and Mail* assignment that would take me right through to the sesquicentennial. The idea was to look at the rivers of Canada in a continuing series that would include photographs, illustrations, and maps. Rivers, after all, were the original highways on this continent, the passageways, often difficult, that allowed First Nations to hunt and trade, that took the first European explorers into the deep country, that allowed the fur trade to flourish, then the timber industry, and that were so critical to transport, power, and settlement.

All Canadians know the importance of rivers to their country, even if this importance is something rarely considered. Ten days before the last federal election, I was sent on short notice to Richmond, BC, for a sit-down interview with the then prime minister, Stephen Harper. I had not been covering the campaign but was tapped by the newspaper to make the journey because of a personal relationship, as a couple of years before a publisher had asked me to help the prime minister shape the historical book on hockey that he was then writing. It was thought I might be able to draw him out, especially as it had become rather obvious that he was in the final days of his nine years in power. When his handlers told me I'd have ten minutes tops with him, any ambitious hopes for a deeply revealing portrait of a political leader at the end of his journey were quickly dashed.

However, the prime minister ignored the time clock and the various hand signals to cut it off – other reporters were lining up for their "one-on-ones." Instead, he changed the subject from himself to what assignment I was working on and he became far more enthusiastic in talking about rivers than he had been about the election. The Harpers had recently purchased property along Bragg Creek, a tributary to the Bow River near Calgary, where they hoped to build a home for their post-Ottawa years.

"I'm very interested in history," the then prime minister said, "and it's often occurred to me that for so much of our history rivers were the centres of everything – life, transportation, trading patterns, you name it. And it's not that they're unimportant now. It's just that they are so less central than they used to be. In fact, we often think now that a river is a pain in the ass to cross, right?

"Well, before, the river was the lifeblood of the entire region. Without a river, there's nothing."

That pretty well summed up the approach we were taking at the *Globe and Mail*. But there would be so much more to it than putting Canada's rivers into some historical perspective. By stressing the original importance of rivers, we could discuss their continuing importance. We could get at sovereignty, climate change, pollution, land claims, fisheries, recreation, and most importantly of all, water quality. The series would serve to remind Canadians that ours is a privileged nation, with more fresh water than any other country in the world. Canada, in fact, has control over an incredible one fifth of the world's fresh water. And with drought threatening Africa and the southwestern U.S., this fresh water becomes more and more valuable with each passing year.

No wonder that, as far back as 2001,

oilman and forty-third president of the United States George W. Bush was saying, "Water is more valuable than oil."

———————————

The "Rivers of Canada" series began with the Red River, which flows from North Dakota up to Winnipeg. The Red is renowned for flooding. Every spring brings warnings, crestings, sandbags, and prayer. In 1997, the waters of the Red spilled out over the flat prairie like a milk pail accidentally kicked over on the barn floor – the usually narrow river suddenly turned into a waterway 40 kilometres wide by 75 kilometres long, with 28,000 people displaced and $400 million suffered in damages. They called it "The Flood of the Century." They could not call it "The Flood of the Millennium" as, it turned out, there had actually been worse flooding the century before. In fact, there have been serious Red River floods recorded in 1826, 1861, 1882, 1897, 1950, 1966, 1969, 1978, 1989, four straight years from 1996 to 1999, 2001, 2006, 2009, 2010, 2011, and 2013. I have covered several of them.

Despite such regular nuisances and a few disasters, Eusebe and Mathilde Courcelles left Quebec in the 1880s and came to homestead at Ste. Agathe on the banks of the Red River, forty kilometres south of Winnipeg. Countless floods and even two lost

homes along the way, the Courcelles family is still there, still holding on to that marvellous Prairie optimism that today can be found in grandson Jacques Courcelles. "My father farmed here for fifty years," he says. "And he believed that every time there was a flood event, he would have a great crop."

It is endlessly fascinating how one part of the country that seems so tied to often-difficult elements would produce such resiliency, even optimism, in the individuals who live there. People undoubtedly change the land they come to. Less considered is how the landscape shapes the people.

We explored the St. Lawrence River that runs from Lake Ontario all the way east to Grosse Île and the gaping Gulf of St. Lawrence, from the surprise of six-storey, 120-room Boldt Castle in the Thousand Islands to the majesty of the Château Frontenac and the boardwalk that sits over Old Quebec. The St. Lawrence is the river of commerce and transportation. It is a river of lost lives (the desperate and sick Irish who put in at Grosse Île) and of changed lives (some 6,500 Canadians displaced, a great many of them reluctantly, from their farms and villages in the 1950s so that the St. Lawrence Seaway could be constructed). But also it has *made* lives, undeniably. Hugh MacLennan, the author of the original publication of *The Colour of Canada*, once wrote that "The St. Lawrence has made

nations. It has been the moulder of lives of millions of people, perhaps by now hundreds of millions, in a multitude of different ways." To him, the river has been "the greatest inland traffic avenue the world has ever known."

In the *Globe and Mail* series, we covered the Muskoka River in Canada's cottage country, and the Niagara River, surely Canada's greatest natural wonder. We paddled and wrote about the Grand River in Southwestern Ontario, with its glorious stone farmhouses and barns. We travelled alongside the Bow River that cascades out of shrinking Bow Glacier in the Rockies, passes through the world-famous town of Banff, and eventually works its way through downtown Calgary. We wrote about the three rivers – the Ottawa, Gatineau, and Rideau – that converge at the nation's capital. We travelled the North Saskatchewan, which crosses the Prairies, and the Columbia River, which twice leaves Canada before emptying into the Pacific Ocean in the American northwest.

No two rivers are the same. What the Saint John River in New Brunswick has in common with, say, the Mackenzie River in the Northwest Territories is . . . water. Explorer Alexander Mackenzie may have called the river that would bear his name "the river of disappointment" – there is some historical debate over whether he actually said that – but today the Mackenzie is regarded as one of the great rivers of the world.

In British Columbia we rode with the search and rescue volunteers of the Hope, BC, fire department up the Fraser River on a 435-horsepower jet boat, the powerful vessel seemingly a bathtub toy as we neared the opening of the Fraser Canyon and the ferocious onslaught of churning whitewater that had come through Hell's Gate. So terrifying is the Fraser at this point that one of the men in the jet boat, Barry Gannon, who has volunteered with the unit for more than thirty years, says they have actually yet to rescue anyone apart from a fly fisher who slipped into the water only a few metres from where the search and rescue unit was launching its boat for a routine practice run. The river, unfortunately, is unforgiving to those who slip, fall, or jump. And yet, downstream from Hope, the "Mighty Fraser" is placid and wide, a river meandering through agricultural lands and small cities until it nears Vancouver, where the waters that once churned white are now so calm people live in small villages of luxury houseboats.

The variety of the country's rivers reflects the variety of the country itself. Canada has salmon rivers, hydroelectric rivers, city rivers, mountain rivers, prairie rivers, cottage rivers, whitewater rivers, and even underground rivers. There are rivers so polluted human waste can be seen floating, and rivers so clean people drink from them.

There is something very special about wild, untouched rivers. The Nahanni River, in the Northwest Territories, is undoubtedly the best known, though the North has many such rivers. Likely most accessible, though, is the Dumoine River, in western Quebec. These are the rivers – perhaps because they remain closest to what existed when First Nations were the only travellers and when the first Europeans arrived – that speak to the very soul of Canada.

There are no dams along the Dumoine, making it unique among the nine major tributaries flowing from western and northern Quebec into the larger Ottawa River. Its power is spiritual rather than electrical.

Legendary canoeist Wally Schaber, founder of the Black Feather wilderness adventures company, has described the Dumoine as "the last of the wild rivers," a wilderness river urban dwellers can easily, and cheaply, reach, a river unsullied by mills or power plants or dams, a river of such exceptional beauty it appears to have been somehow misplaced on the Canadian map. But no, it is not flowing somewhere in the territories. So much of Canada's great beauty is inaccessible, but sometimes we forget how much is accessible.

"The great beauty of a river trip," Schaber says, "is you don't have to navigate – you just follow the water."

And that is essentially what Sandford Fleming set out to do in 1872. Five years after Confederation had created this new entity known as "Canada," the Scottish-born Fleming – who would become the inventor of worldwide standard time zones – was put in charge of an expedition that would make its way across the newly joined colonies and acquired territories to see just what had come of all that big talk in Charlottetown and Quebec City.

The group travelled from Halifax all the way to Victoria. They calculated, in the measurements of the day, that they had covered 1,687 miles by steamer; 2,185 miles by horse power, including coaches, wagons, packs, and saddle-horses; nearly 1,000 miles by train; and 485 miles in canoes or rowboats. Rivers, not surprisingly, had proved as vital to these post-Confederation travellers as they had to the early explorers and First Nations.

George Monro Grant, the Halifax preacher and Confederation booster assigned to keep a written record of the great Fleming expedition, described what a previous traveller had called "The Great Lone Land."[1] The landscape, Grant wrote – awe-inspiring and intimidating at the same time – "rolled out before us like a panorama, varied and magnificent enough to stir the dullest spirit into patriotic emotion."[2]

This has never really changed. In 1944, more than seven decades after Grant observed the spiritually powerful experience of travelling through the Canadian landscape, a young Montreal academic named Pierre Trudeau penned an essay he titled "Exhaustion and Fulfillment: The Ascetic in a Canoe." "Travel a thousand miles by train," the future prime minister wrote, "and you are a brute; pedal five hundred on a bicycle and you remain basically a bourgeois; paddle a hundred in a canoe and you are already a child of nature."

One of Trudeau's great paddling pals was Blair Fraser, the popular Ottawa editor of *Maclean's* magazine. During the country's last significant birthday, the 1967 centennial year, Fraser published *The Search for Identity*, in which he argued that "What held [early settlers] together was not love for each other, but love for the land itself, the vast, empty land in which, for more than three centuries, a certain kind of man has found himself uniquely at home."

It was a deft observation about how Canadian men – and women – think of their vast and impossible land. Fraser surely would have had much more to say about this relationship had he lived longer, but only months after the centennial year he was dead, drowned at fifty-nine after the

---

1   William Francis Butler. *The Great Lone Land*. London: Sampson Low, Marston, Low, & Searle, 1872.

2   George Monro Grant. *Ocean to Ocean*. Toronto: James Campbell & Son, 1873.

canoe he was paddling was swept into the Rollway Rapids on the Petawawa River.

While it was an unspeakable tragedy to his family and friends, there was something apt about this man dying in the Canadian Shield, which he had often written of so eloquently. Back in December 1955, Fraser had written in *Maclean's* that "One of the things that make our country what it is, a little different from most other countries however similar or however friendly, is the awareness that the wilderness is not far away. However urban we become, however soft and civilized, we still have the cleansing wild within a hundred miles more or less. It is good to know that no matter how much richer and stronger we may grow, Canada will still be the same kind of country."[3]

Fast forward to the summer of 2003, when the newspaper I was working for was running an extended series on multiculturalism tagged "New Canada." The *Globe and Mail* commissioned a poll to ask citizens what, to their minds, best symbolized the country in which they lived, whether they had been born there or had come to it from elsewhere. While the hope might have been that they would choose "multiculturalism," such concepts as "medicare," "hockey," "maple syrup,"

"moose," "snow," and "Tim Hortons" were obvious possibilities. But no, none of these came near the top spot. Instead, a remarkable 89 per cent of those surveyed chose the sheer "vastness of the land."

In Canada, size matters.

———————————————

But so, too, does smallness. I do not quite understand Herman Melville's sentiment in *Moby Dick* – "It's not down on any map; true places never are" – but I do have a soft spot for special places and semi-secret places. That, too, is the Canada we love and treasure as much as any concept of the "vastness" of the land itself.

There is, for example, a magical place on the eastern border of Ontario's Algonquin Provincial Park where it appears nature paused to make something special for children and those who make every effort to fight growing up. Canoe trippers heading down the Barron Canyon, a spectacular sight on its own, will suspend their paddle after Stratton Lake for a couple of hours or more to stop at High Falls. When the last glaciers retreated from this area twelve thousand years ago, they gouged out a playground in the granite, forming large "bowls" of stone where the warm waters of summer shift from one gouged-out hollow to the next in long, smooth rock slides. It is almost as if there should be hidden hydraulics causing

3   Blair Fraser, "The Fairy Tale Romance of the Canadian Shield," *Maclean's*, December 1955, 42-45.

the effect, but in fact, it is nature at its most inventive, most amazing. Children of all ages can slide from one bowl to the other. They can rest in a bubbling "hot tub" that is neither hot nor cold but flushed with water so remarkably fresh and clean your skin tingles for hours after hauling yourself and your group away from this natural play structure and back onto your canoe trek to the canyon and beyond.

If High Falls were in America, it would be called something like the Rock Bowl Theme Park, with shuttle buses taking people to the ticket booths and signs posted on the path to the falls saying things like "90 minutes to the first slide." But this is Canada, where the magical spot is almost kept a secret by those who have found it, their instructions on how to get there written on paper that must be eaten once the lucky have reached their near-secret destination.

There is a small outport on the east coast of Newfoundland, just north of Terra Nova National Park, where, on the drive out from the Trans-Canada Highway through Traytown and Eastport, you begin to think you have entered another country – as if Newfoundland and Labrador itself were not different enough from the rest of Canada. Eventually you will come to the village of Salvage, a settlement that goes back beyond the Basque fishermen to the Beothuks. The 174 lucky people who live there

today may have the finest seascape view in North America, one often graced with the latest entry in that long parade of floats known as Iceberg Alley.

There is a walk near the small town of Fairmont Hot Springs, in British Columbia, that heads up from the west side of Columbia Lake toward the Purcell Mountains, where, after a few twists and turns that allow you to see all the way across the valley to the magnificent Rocky Mountains to the east, you will come across dozens of spectacular "hoodoos" carved into the sand by nothing other than the natural elements. It is almost mystical.

If you were to leave the Trans-Canada Highway around Regina and head north on Saskatchewan Highway 6, you would eventually fall off the table. There is no other way to describe it. For as far as the eye can see, the brown prairie seems flat, the highway stretching on forever – then, suddenly, there is no highway at all in front of you. You "fall off" the prairie into the Qu'Appelle Valley, a breathtaking fissure in the landscape where the highway drops far down, then heads along the valley bottom, bridging the little Qu'Appelle River before rising again on the other side to resume the flat journey north. Those who choose to drive, instead, along the river will come to know what the Mohawk poet E. Pauline Johnson meant when she wrote

I am the one who heard the spirit voice,
Of which the paleface settlers love to tell;
From whose strange story they have
   made their choice
Of naming this fair valley the
   "Qu'Appelle."

Farther on up Highway 6 the road north intersects with Highway 15 running east and west. Highway 6 began as an old trail that followed the Grand Trunk Pacific Railway as it expanded west, and so the water and fuel stops that eventually became small communities were named in alphabetical order: "Punnichy, Quinton, Raymore, Semans, Tate, Undora, Venn, Watrous, Xena, Young, Zelma . . ." While Watrous has become a town of some two thousand, others, like Tate, are now ghost towns. It happened slowly for Tate – the post office closing in 1968, the village no longer found on provincial maps a decade later – and a few years ago a teenage graduation party got out of control and the few remaining buildings still standing were burned to the ground.

That does not mean Tate no longer exists, of course. There is the immaculately maintained graveyard tended by volunteers, most of whom once lived in the village or are the children of "Taters." Each summer a reunion is held near the cemetery. Tailgates come down, barbeques and salads come forth, and the people walk about, remembering. "This is my father and mother," one elderly man

told me a decade ago when I dropped in on one of the Tate reunions. "And over here's my brother." He was introducing me to tombstones.

There is a sense of place found in the Prairies that would take issue with Mackenzie King's line about too much geography and too little history. When U.S. author Wallace Stegner returned briefly to Eastend, the tiny southern Saskatchewan community where he spent his formative years – and which inspired him to write his best-known work, *Wolf Willow* – he noted that such places, so far removed from any ocean, are oddly like a "coral reef" in that they accumulate through the "slow accrual" of time, life, birth, death, and memory. The sense of place so rock solid it never seems to vanish.

A few kilometres east from Tate along the alphabetical rail line brings you to Raymore, a now-thriving community near where my mother-in-law's family homesteaded before Saskatchewan became a province in 1905. Their first mail, sent over from relatives in England, was addressed to the Northwest Territories. The two originals, J.E. Whitlock and his wife, Ellen, lived on the homestead until their ninety-eighth years, the two of them passing away within a few months of each other. The farm then fell to their bachelor sons, Ted and Fred. Fred Whitlock could, and would, recite all ninety lines of Pauline Johnson's ode to the Qu'Appelle and never miss a beat. Fred, a Second World War air force navigator who survived the crash landing of his Wellington bomber into the Mediterranean, had his small, special place, too – a field back of the farm where a huge rock, presumably fumbled by the last glacier passing through, lay like a giant throne. Fred liked to go there and sit. Nothing else. Just sit and contemplate the amazing, totally unknown country his parents had come to a century earlier.

Billy Diamond, the great leader of the James Bay Cree in northern Quebec, had an off-shore camp he would retreat to during the spring goose hunt. It was here, on McLean Island in a snow blind back on April 28, 1971, that the young newly elected chief of Rupert House had sat playing with the transistor radio he had brought home from his high-school graduation in Sault Ste. Marie and was able to tune in the CBC's *World at Six*. The news out of Quebec was the coming announcement of the "project of the century," a six-billion-dollar hydroelectric project that would provide 125,000 jobs and would mean the damming up of the rivers that poured through the Crees' traditional hunting and trapping territories. No one had even bothered to ask the Cree.

Billy Diamond's long court battle led to the ground-breaking James Bay Agreement, Canada's first modern treaty, which today is held up as the first successful example of self-government in Canada. Years later, the grand chief of the James Bay Cree, who passed away in 2010 at the relatively young age of sixty-one, still liked nothing better than to return to McLean Island – only then he came to tune *out* the world.

As North American nature writer John A. Murray once so perfectly put it, "Every so often a disappearance is in order. A vanishing. A checking out. An indeterminate period of unavailability." Another American writer, Marjorie Kinnan Rawlings, famous for her novel *The Yearling*, has said, "I do not understand how anyone can live without some small place of enchantment to turn to."

Such places of enchantment are throughout this book of photography. They can be found everywhere in Canada, special places that visiting tourists often seem to treasure as much as Canadians themselves. Sometimes you just need to "get away."

Call it "basic rhythm," "cabin fever," whatever, it is a fact of life, one so ingrained in the Canadian culture that more than a half century ago Manitoba historian W.L. Morton noted that the "alternative penetration of the wilderness and return to civilization is the basic rhythm of Canadian life."

And it remains so.

There is no doubt that terrain and climate can intimidate – the settling of Canada was a long and difficult process – but there is a beauty in ruggedness and rich variety in weather, as many of the photographs in this book will show. Even so, it took time for the elements to be appreciated. Jacques Cartier, the early explorer who claimed this unforgiving land for the King of France, was close to giving up after the first winter here killed a quarter of his men. A later explorer, Alexander Mackenzie, once wrote back to Scotland, "I begin to think this is the height of folly in a man to reside in a country of this kind deprived of every comfort that can render life agreeable."

Canadians have long been sensitive about their winters. Voltaire, remember, dismissed us as "a few acres of snow." British prime minister William Gladstone kissed us off as the land "of perpetual ice and snow." British tabloid journalists still regularly call us that "Great White Waste of Time." When British writer Frances Brooke came to the colony with her clergyman husband in 1763, she quickly concluded, "Genius will never mount high here where the faculties of the mind are benumbed half the year."

There was a time when the Canadian government was so prickly about such slagging that, at one point when seeking to attract European immigrants to take up land in the Prairies, the word *cold* was banned from all printed materials – to be replaced with the more acceptable *buoyant*.

"There is a beauty in ruggedness and rich variety in weather."

But no more. Canadians now embrace the elements – in part thanks to new, lightweight materials for winter clothing – and find as much beauty in snow as in sunshine. We are never so confident a nation as when the Winter Olympic Games are on. Today, winter is us.

But if there was once a misconception about how we live, there remains one about *where* we live. On any given day of the week, someone on Canadian television or in a Canadian newspaper will say or write that "80 per cent of Canadians live in cities." It is a phrase repeated so often it has become accepted wisdom and not only affects our perception of the country in which we live but can, and does, have a profound influence on policy. If the rural population of Canada amounts to but one in five, do

those people really count all that much?

Unfortunately, the figure is wrong and misleading.

The fault lies, in part, with a government agency that Canadians should, no pun intended, be able to count on: Statistics Canada. The rest of the fault lies with the media. The problem has its genesis in the definition of *urban area*, which goes all the way back to 1861, six years before Confederation, when the governments of Canada East and Canada West determined, quite acceptably given the times, that any place with one thousand people could be deemed "urban." Over the decades, the definition was tweaked many times to link that thousand-citizen cut-off to a specific area measurement, but the definition stood – making places such as Arnold's Cove, Newfoundland and Labrador; Barry's Bay, Ontario; Birch Hills, Saskatchewan; and Bernierville, Quebec, "urban" in the eyes of Statistics Canada. By this sadly out-of-date definition, 80 per cent of Canadians do indeed live in "urban" centres. The media, to make matters worse, see the word *urban*, transform it into *city*, and we end up with a continuing misread of the reality of this country.

In recent years, some politicians took up the misconception and demanded that Statistics Canada bring its definitions more in line with the reality of Canada. Tony Clement, the long-time Conservative member of Parliament for Parry Sound–Muskoka, an Ontario riding with numerous "urban" small towns, and Keith Martin, up until the 2011 federal election a Liberal member for the British Columbia riding of Esquimalt–Juan de Fuca, were two politicians who took up the argument with some success. Martin once called it "an artificial divide – and it preys on old mythologies of people in rural areas being hewers of wood and drawers of water, whereas 'urban' people are more sophisticated and higher educated. Those stereotypes are long gone."

Finally, Statistics Canada did bow to the pressure and tweaked its definitions yet again in 2011. Places like little Barry's Bay would henceforth no longer be designated "urban areas" but "population centres." "Small population centre" would cover those with populations 1,000 to 29,999, "medium" those between 30,000 and 99,999, and "large" those with 100,000 or more. It was a welcome change, but by then the notion that "80 per cent of Canadians live in cities" was as solid a national belief as "Canadians apologize too much."

Sorry about that – but it's true.

It is difficult to say what is an accurate definition of where Canadians live. If a true city is considered to be, say, 100,000, then we might state that just over half of Canadians live in cities. If your notion of a city is, say, Orillia, Ontario, population 30,000, then it might be fair to say that roughly two thirds of Canadians live in cities – a rather different view of who we are and where we live than the erroneous four out of five that the media cling to so stubbornly. We are indeed an urbanized society, but we are also rural, in psychological measures as well as physical – and proudly so.

I count myself fortunate for the amount of time I have been privileged to spend travelling about this country with professional photographers. Once I stood in the cold Miramichi River in New Brunswick suspending a fish aquarium that held an expensive camera just below the river's surface while the *Globe and Mail*'s John Lehmann took remote shots of a fly fisher bringing in a fat salmon. With wonderful photojournalists like Fred Lum, Kevin Van Paassen, and Brian Willer, I have flown and driven and snowmobiled through the Far North, visited the isolated Cree villages along the eastern coast of James Bay, and crossed the Maritimes with the Olympic torch relay. Their photographs, time and time again, have been worth a million words, not a thousand.

Writers often say that good writing is good rewriting. You go back again and again. So, too, it is with photography; that miraculous shot that catches the light just right or frames the subject just so is not a matter of luck – though the photograph is even better if seen as such – but of planning, patience, and often persistence. I recall one northern excursion with Fred Lum in 2006 when we had spent the day in Behchoko, a Dogrib community on the northwest tip of Great Slave Lake in the Northwest Territories. I had done several interviews and Fred had spent the day shooting hundreds of photographs of the village and its people. We were about fifty kilometres into our drive back to Yellowknife when, suddenly, Fred asked me to turn around.

"I have to go back," he said.

"*What for?*" I asked. I had everything I needed, and more. He had hundreds of photographs.

"I still haven't got the shot I need," he said.

Rather miffed – I'd been thinking of a cold beer back at the place where we were staying – I agreed to Fred's strange request, and back we headed to Behchoko.

His instincts turned out to be right. Once there, we were passing by a small trailer and shed when something caught his eye. We stopped in and found Elisabeth Chocolate, an eighty-year-old elder, busy scraping the fat from a beaver pelt. She was using a traditional tool, a sort of knife fashioned from the leg of a caribou. While Elisabeth worked and told

Glacier Skywalk, Jasper National Park, Alberta

stories of growing up on traplines, her son-in-law, Patrick Adzin, translating for us, Fred took more and more photographs, finally getting what he knew he needed for our feature.

There is a very special connection between this country and the camera lens, whether the images belong to a professional photojournalist like Fred Lum, a selfie-taking busload of tourists along the Columbia Icefields Parkway, or a visiting adventurer who has come by passenger jet, bush plane, canoe, and foot to find the one shot that will make his or her expensive trip into the Canadian wilderness worthwhile. Obviously, many have concluded the trip is worth the cost, whether it be group tour or individual adventure.

Canada's national parks have seen the number of visitors rise in recent years to roughly 13.5 million, nearly 8 million of those visitors choosing the vistas of the seven national parks that feature mountains. Whether this popularity reflects a deep love of nature or the low value of the Canadian dollar – no doubt both are factors – the number of foreign visitors to Canada has been on a steady rise. And the one hundred and fiftieth birthday party will no doubt bring in even more tourists who will reach for their cameras as soon as the

vehicle comes to a stop, if not before.

What attracts these foreign visitors to Canada varies widely, but I shall never forget a conversation I had at Smoke Lake in Algonquin Park with a visitor from the Netherlands. Making small talk, I merely asked him what was the best thing he had seen during his visit, thinking that he would mention a moose, perhaps a black bear, possibly even a wolf. "Well, you know," he said, "I have never in my life been the only car I can see on the road." It took me a moment to realize what he was saying, but then I understood. In Europe, the open road is inconceivable. In much of Canada, the open road is the usual.

And that, perhaps, is what evokes this vast country best: the open road. The endless possibilities. When Bruce Hutchison was finishing up *The Unknown Country* and took his own look down the path his country was headed, he found himself filled with optimism. "Wondrous and very sweet is our name. *Canada!*" he wrote. "The very word is like a boy's shout in the springtime, is like the clamour of geese going north and the roar of melting rivers and the murmur of early winds."

Bruce Hutchison was able to see his country reach its one hundredth birthday in 1967, a year that forever hangs in the Canadian memory as a magical time of endless possibilities. He died in 1992 at the age of ninety-one, worried terribly about his country, which was then going through constitutional throes that, for a time, seemed to threaten the very existence of the country.

He would be mightily pleased, then, to behold the country on its hundred and fiftieth birthday. Canada might be a bit of a "bumblebee" nation – hard to say how it manages to fly so well, yet it does – but it now stands as the world's second-oldest federation, after only the United States. Not only that, but as the eve of 2017 approached, the World Economic Forum in Davos, Switzerland, declared Canada the number one country in the world when it comes to quality of life.

Author Peter C. Newman once tagged Hutchison as "the eternal optimist" and he had good reason for such a sunny outlook. Canada is deservedly renowned for its tolerance and for its ability to integrate newcomers – the arrival of thousands of Syrian refugees being just the latest example. As Prime Minister Justin Trudeau said when he greeted the first arrivals who landed in Toronto, "You are home – welcome home."

"There is a very special connection between this country and the camera lens."

And as Bruce Hutchison said on behalf of these people who would arrive seventy-five years later, "Wondrous and very sweet is our name. *Canada!*" This country is no longer "unknown," though it may be "unknowable."

Perhaps it is in this quality that the true beauty and attraction of Canada can be found.

For surely we are the only 150-year-old country in the world that is still being discovered.

THE TER

Bleak, beautiful, captivating – the Canadian North with its breathtaking vastness is proof that a country 150 years old is still being explored.

RITORIES

Dawson City, Yukon

Great Slave Lake, Northwest Territories

North of Baffin Island, Nunavut

Richardson Mountains, Northwest Territories

Arctic Ocean, north of Baffin Island, Nunavut

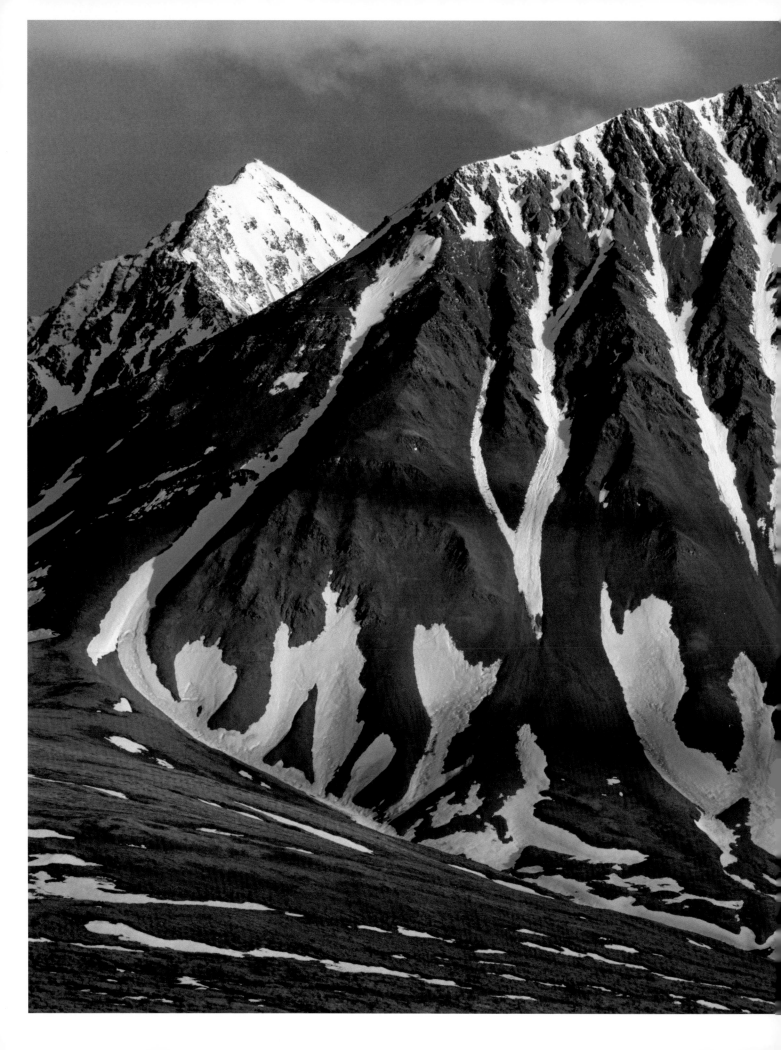

St. Elias Mountains, Haines Junction, Yukon

Barren Lands, central Northwest Territories

Giant Mine townsite, Northwest Territories

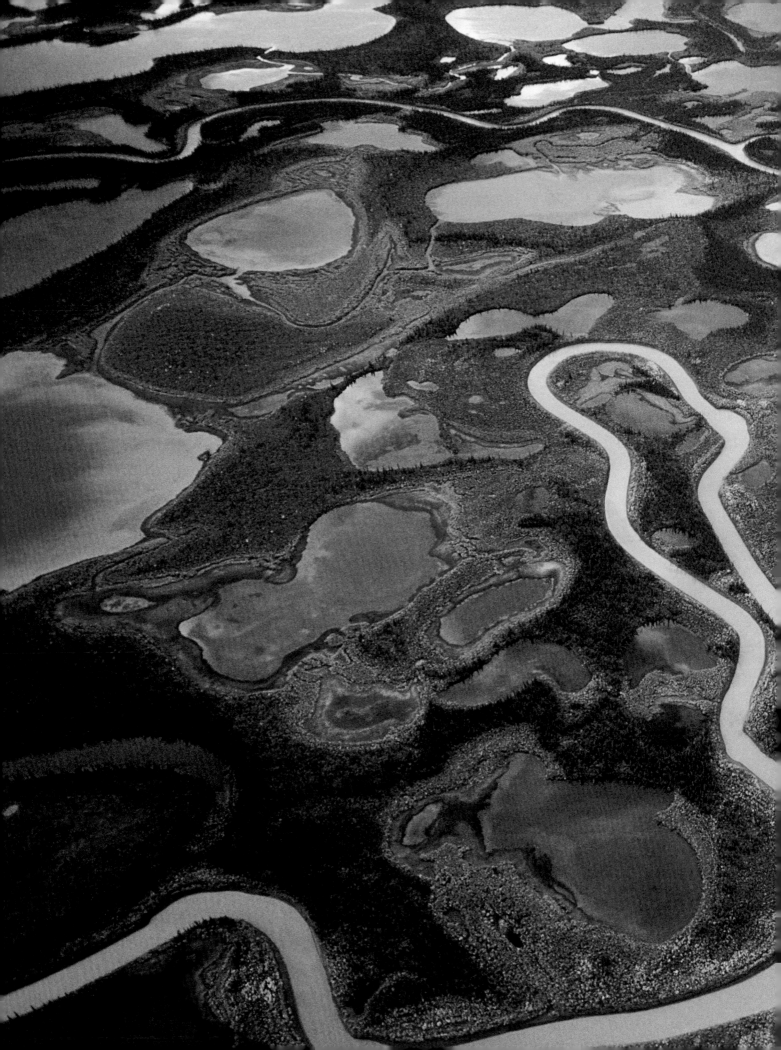

Mackenzie Delta, Northwest Territories

Ekati Diamond Mine, north of Yellowknife, Northwest Territories

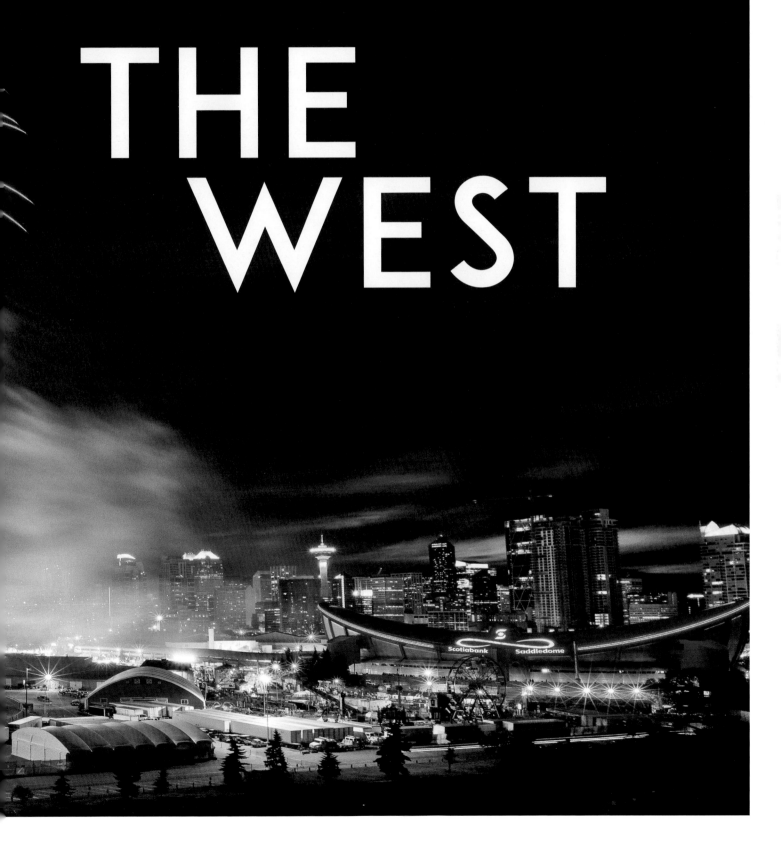

The energy source of Canada in far more ways than the obvious – where tomorrow is forever.

THE
WEST

Calgary Stampede, Calgary, Alberta

Capilano Suspension Bridge, totem pole detail, North Vancouver, British Columbia

Lions Gate Bridge, Vancouver, British Columbia

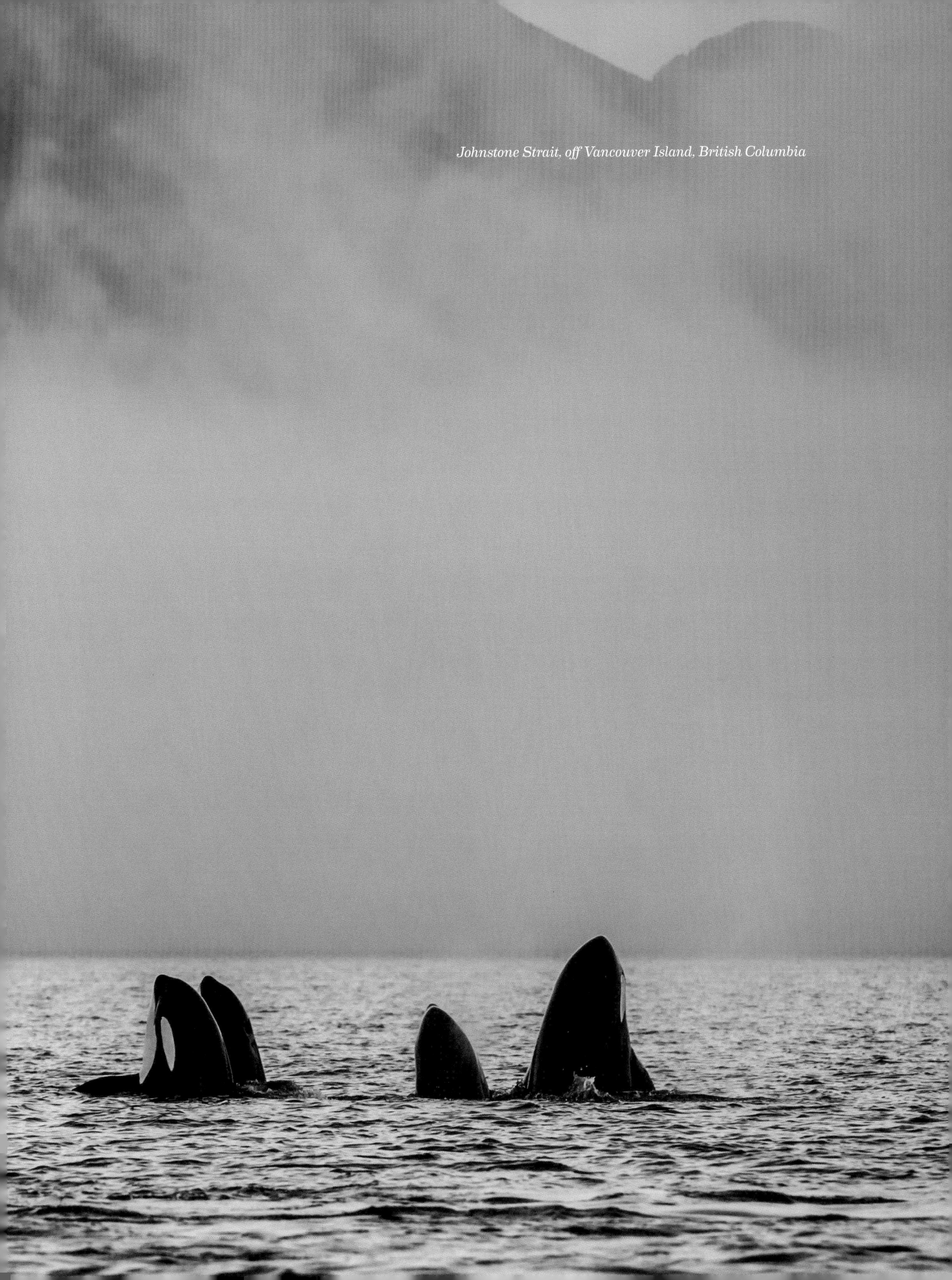

Johnstone Strait, off Vancouver Island, British Columbia

Chinatown gate, Edmonton, Alberta

Gastown, Vancouver, British Columbia

Capilano Suspension Bridge, Vancouver, British Columbia

Kendrick Arm log dump, British Columbia

Stanley Park seawall, Vancouver, British Columbia

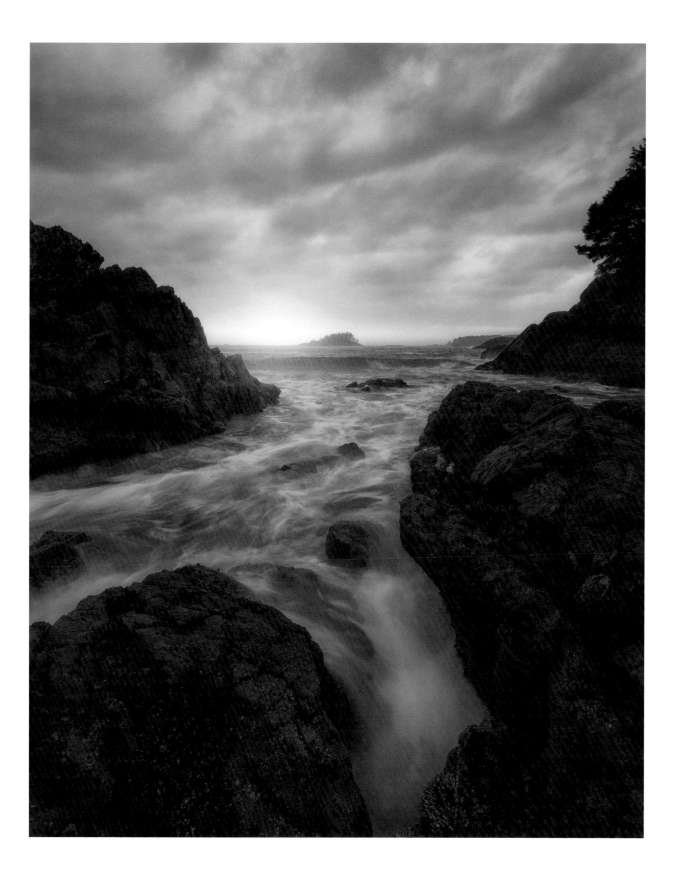

Tofino, British Columbia

Spotted Lake, Similkameen Valley, British Columbia

Quartzite boulder pile, Jasper National Park, Alberta

Drumheller, Alberta

THE PRAIRIES

Big skies and big hearts. It is here where the core values of Canadians –

cooperation, acceptance, tolerance – were born and where they remain strongest today.

Big Muddy Badlands, Saskatchewan

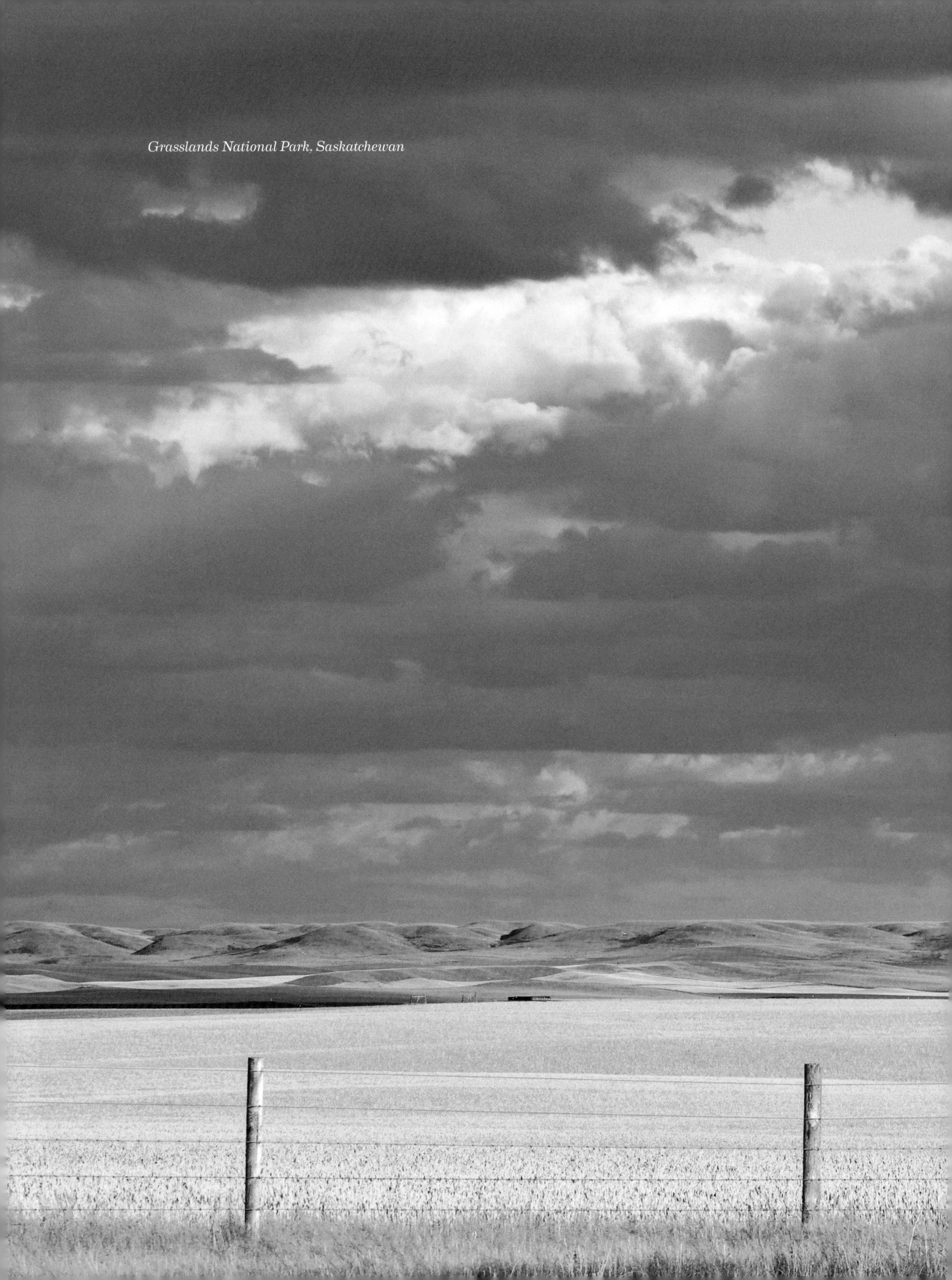

Grasslands National Park, Saskatchewan

St. Leon, Manitoba

Lake Winnipeg, Gimli, Manitoba

The Crossing Resort, Grasslands National Park, Saskatchewan

Red River, Esplanade Riel Bridge, and Canadian Museum for Human Rights, Winnipeg, Manitoba

Churchill, Manitoba

The Great Ice Show, Winnipeg, Manitoba

Stick Pier, Lake Winnipeg. Matlock, Manitoba

Biggest city, biggest population, biggest economy – yet a place filled with small surprises and treasures. If size matters, it does so in both directions.

ONTARIO

Sault Ste. Marie, Ontario

Don Valley Parkway, Toronto, Ontario

Lake of the Woods, Northwestern Ontario

Rideau Canal, Ottawa, Ontario

Fort Henry Guard, Upper Canada Village, Morrisburg, Ontario

Distillery District, Toronto, Ontario

Art Gallery of Ontario, Toronto, Ontario

City Hall, Toronto, Ontario

Canadian Shield, Georgian Bay, Ontario

Horseshoe Falls, Niagara Falls, Ontario

Agawa Canyon Wilderness Park. Ontario

The essence of what makes Canada unique – a vibrant, spectacular province where one hand holds onto the past while the other reaches for the future.

QUEBEC

Trois Pistoles, Quebec

Montreal Convention Centre, Montreal, Quebec

Mont-Tremblant National Park, Laurentides, Quebec

FRAMBOISES
7 ⁰⁰

Bleuets
sauvages
Abitibi !
* 6 ⁰⁰ *

Jean-Talon Market, Montreal, Quebec

Caprivoix Farm, Charlevoix, Quebec

Montreal Tower, Olympic Park, Montreal, Quebec

Old Montreal, Quebec

Percé Rock, Gaspé Peninsula, Quebec

Quebec City, Quebec

Magdalen Islands, L'Étang-du-Nord, Quebec

THE MARITIMES

Postcard Country – a place of gentle pleasures, warm people, pastoral landscapes, and, best of all, slightly slower clocks.

POLLY

North Head, Grand Manan Island, New Brunswick

VI

V

IV

Bluenose II, *Halifax, Nova Scotia*

Jude's Point, Prince Edward Island

Fogo Island, Newfoundland and Labrador

Peggy's Cove, Nova Scotia

Confederation Bridge, Borden-Carleton, Prince Edward Island

Prince Edward Island National Park

Green Gables, Cavendish, Prince Edward Island

Halifax, Nova Scotia

Twillingate, Newfoundland and Labrador

Greenspond, Newfoundland and Labrador

ABOUT THE AUTHOR

Roy MacGregor is the acclaimed and bestselling author of *Northern Light: The Enduring Mystery of Tom Thomson and the Woman Who Loved Him*; *Home Team: Fathers, Sons and Hockey* (shortlisted for the Governor General's Literary Award); *A Life in the Bush* (winner of the U.S. Rutstrum Award for Best Wilderness Book and the CAA Award for Biography); *Canadians: A Portrait of a Country and Its People*; *Wayne Gretzky's Ghost: And Other Tales from a Lifetime in Hockey*; as well as two novels, *Canoe Lake* and *The Last Season*, and the popular Screech Owls mystery series for young readers. A long-time columnist at *The Globe and Mail*, MacGregor has won four National Magazine Awards and two National Newspaper Awards. He is an Officer of the Order of Canada, and was described in the citation as one of Canada's "most gifted storytellers."

IMAGE CREDITS

Hardcover edition published 2017

McClelland & Stewart and colophon are registered trademarks of McClelland & Stewart

Library and Archives Canada Cataloguing in Publication

MacGregor, Roy, 1948-, author

    The colour of Canada / with text by Roy MacGregor.

Issued in print and electronic formats.

ISBN 978-0-7710-2398-9 (hardback).—ISBN 978-0-7710-2399-6 (epub)

    1. Canada—Pictorial works. I. All Canada Photos II. Title.

FC59.M328 2017   971.0022'2   C2016-904558-7

                                      C2016-904559-5

Jacket art: (front) Dave Blackey/All Canada Photos; (back) Michael Wheatley/All Canada Photos

Printed case art: Terry A. Parker/All Canada Photos

Endpaper art: Chris Cheadle/All Canada Photos

Typeset in Eames Century Modern by M&S, Toronto

Printed and bound in Canada

McClelland & Stewart,

a division of Penguin Random House Canada Limited,

a Penguin Random House Company

www.penguinrandomhouse.ca

1 2 3 4 5   21 20 19 18 17

Penguin
Random
House